Marbles
Roller
Skates
Doorknobs

Marbles
Roller Skates
Doorknobs

SIMPLE MACHINES THAT ARE REALLY **WHEELS**

BY CHRISTOPHER LAMPTON
PICTURES BY CAROL NICKLAUS

THE MILLBROOK PRESS • BROOKFIELD, CT
A GATEWAY BOOK

Cataloging-in-Publication Data

Lampton, Christopher
Marbles, roller skates and doorknobs /
Christopher Lampton; pictures by Carol Nicklaus
Brookfield, CT., Millbrook Press, 1991.
32 p. : ill.
Includes glossary and index.
ISBN 1–878841–24–6
1. Simple Machines.   2. Wheels.
3. Science - Experiments.   I. Title.   II. Carol Nicklaus, ill.

Where would we be without wheels?

Cars couldn't move without wheels. Wind-up watches wouldn't keep time without wheels. Without wheels there would be no bicycles, record players, or roller coasters.

You never know where you are going to find a wheel. There are wheels in file drawers, photocopying machines, and computer disk drives. Look inside a dishwasher and you'll see wheels. Office chairs roll on wheels. Blenders use wheels to make milk shakes. . . .

All those wheels are enough to make your head spin!

You don't have to be a scientist to figure out what wheels do. But have you ever thought about how many kinds of wheels there are and the different ways in which they work?

When you think of a wheel, you probably think of the type that is on a car or a wagon. But did you know that a ball can be a wheel? Or that there is a kind of wheel with teeth? Don't worry. It won't bite you. It's called a **gear,** and it's usually found inside a machine.

Wheels make it easier to move things. If you don't believe this, pull your wagon across the grass. Then turn it upside down and try to pull it. As we said, wheels make it easier to move things!

To explore the difference wheels make, first imagine pulling a heavy load on a sled through the snow. You might huff and puff a little, but you can do it. What would happen if you came to a road with no snow on it? Could you pull the sled across it? Probably not.

Now think about what would happen if you attached wheels to the sled. You would have no problem pulling it—heavy load and all—across even a rough road. The wheels make this possible.

Let's see how a ball can be a wheel and make it easier to move things. Put a marble on a smooth floor and give it a push. It keeps rolling in a straight line until it bumps against something.

Now put a flat-bottomed box on the floor. Give it a push and notice what happens.

What makes the box come to a stop while the marble keeps rolling?

Now put some marbles under the box and try moving it around on the floor. Can you feel how wheels make it easier for you to move the box? Why is this so?

To answer these questions, first note how the floor resists the movement of the box. This resistance is called **friction.** The amount of friction depends on the weight of the box and the roughness of the surfaces of the box and the floor. In the case of the box, there is so much friction that the box won't move very far at all.

The marble, on the other hand, rolls a long way across the floor. There isn't as much friction when one object rolls over another. So, when we need to cut down on friction to help something move faster, we often use a wheel.

In fact, ball-shaped wheels are so effective at reducing friction that they are placed between the moving parts of many machines. Tiny metal balls called **ball bearings** keep various moving parts inside automobiles from rubbing against one another. When you roller skate, you are getting a double dose of wheels. You are, of course, skating on wheels, thereby reducing the friction against the road. But wheels are also operating *inside* the wheels of your skates. Ball bearings are reducing the friction inside of the wheels so that they will turn more smoothly.

We have learned one important way in which wheels help us: they reduce friction so that we can move things more easily. But wheels do more for us than this.

Sometimes a wheel is connected to a rod that turns with it. This rod is called the **axle.** Together, the wheel and axle form what is called a **simple machine.**

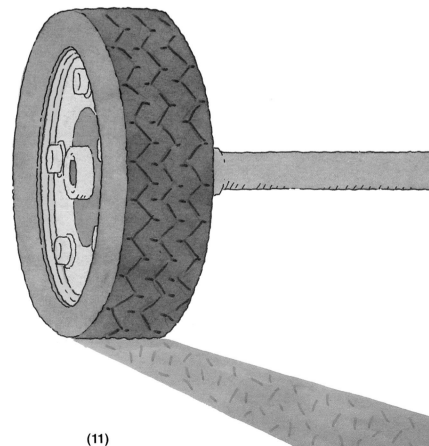

When you think of machines, you probably think of things like bulldozers and clothes dryers and automobiles. These are machines too, but they are **complex machines.** The reason simple machines are so important is that all complex machines are combinations of simple machines.

Complex machines are often powered by electricity or gasoline. They do work for us. You can turn on a dishwasher and come back later to find your dishes washed. Simple machines usually require some muscle power from us, but they may be powered. A screwdriver is a simple machine that requires muscle power. An electric screwdriver is powered.

The wheel alone reduces friction to help us move things. But the wheel and axle, like other simple machines, helps us to accomplish work. You certainly know how it feels to be tired out from doing work, but you may not have thought about how scientists define work.

To find the amount of work performed, you first measure the amount of effort, or force, you must use to move something. Then you measure the distance over which you must apply that force. By multiplying the force times the distance, you can calculate what scientists define as the amount of work performed. In other words, **Force $\times$ Distance = Work.**

Let's make a wheel and axle to observe this relationship between force and distance in action.

Find a plastic lid, such as the kind used on a coffee can or a can of nuts. This will serve as your wheel. Now, stick a pencil through the center of the lid. Roll the pencil between your fingers. By turning the axle (the pencil) a little, you can make the wheel (the lid) turn a lot. You can get a lot of motion out of just a little motion.

Make a mark on the rim of the lid in line with the side of the pencil that has writing on it. Roll the pencil slowly between your fingers until it makes one complete turn. The mark on the rim of the wheel travels much farther than the writing on the pencil.

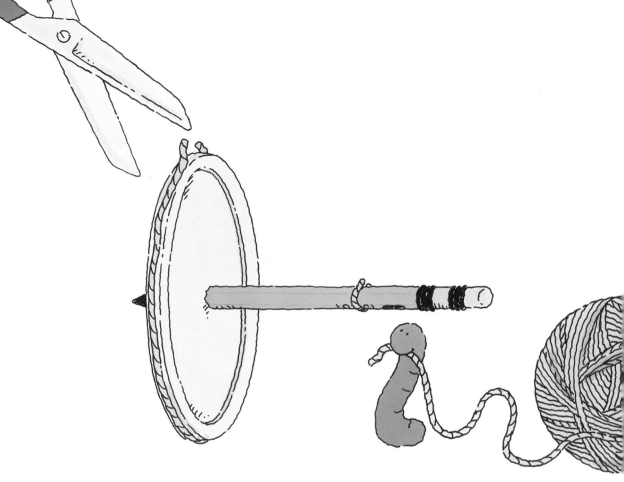

Here's an experiment to give you a more precise measurement of how much farther the rim of the wheel travels than the axle. Tape the end of a piece of string to the rim of the lid. Wind the string around the rim to measure the distance around the wheel, cutting the string at the point where it circles the wheel once. Measure the distance around the axle (the pencil) with a piece of string in the same way. Then, lay the two strings side by side.

See how much longer the first string is than the second string? The length of the first string shows how far a point on the rim of the wheel travels as it goes around one turn. The second string shows how far a point on the axle travels as it goes around one turn.

But how does the distance that a point travels on a wheel or an axle relate to the amount of effort you use to get work done? Remember that effort times distance equals the amount of work accomplished.

THIS STRING IS MUCH LONGER

Let's continue with our experiments to explore effort.

Tie a piece of string securely to your pencil. Then tie a toy truck, or anything that weighs one pound or so, to the other end of the string. This will be the load.

Holding your pencil near one end, turn the other end of the pencil to raise the load. The string will wind around the axle (the pencil). (Tape the string to the pencil if it slips.) Notice the amount of effort it took to lift the load.

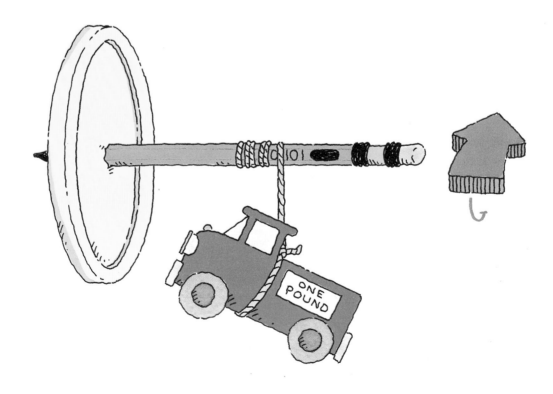

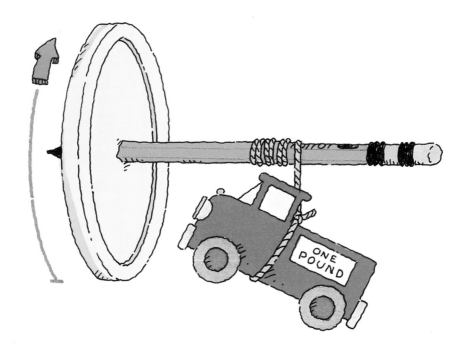

Now repeat the experiment, but this time turn the wheel (the lid) instead of the axle (the pencil). Notice how much less force you used to turn the wheel than to turn the axle. But notice how much farther you had to move it. As you can see, there is a **trade-off.** You turned the wheel farther but you used less force.

The amount of force you need to do a job depends on the size of the wheel and the size of the axle. So, if a wheel is 10 inches around and an axle is 1 inch around, you need only one tenth of the force when you turn the wheel to lift the load. In other words, the greater the distance you have to cover, the less force you need to move the load.

Can you think of an everyday situation in which we would want to use less force to turn the outside rim of a wheel, thereby creating a stronger force at the axle?

Think about what happens when you turn a doorknob to open a door. The two door knobs on either side of the door are really two wheels connected by an axle. The axle is a small metal bar that must turn in order to operate the door mechanism. You probably would not have the strength to turn that axle by holding it directly with your hands, but you can turn the wheel—the doorknob, that is—and open the door.

Have you ever seen a water faucet with the handle removed? There's just a metal rod sticking out that has to be turned in order to turn the water on and off. It is very difficult to turn the rod with your bare hands. But by applying much less force to the faucet handle, you can easily move the axle underneath it. You're making a trade-off by turning the wheel a greater distance to get more force from the axle.

At other times we have lots of force available, but we want to move something as great a distance as possible. So, instead of trading distance for force, we trade force for distance. Take the case of the automobile, for example. The engine supplies us with lots of force, and in exchange for that force, the wheels give us lots of distance.

We have seen how a wheel and axle allows us to trade force for distance or distance for force. When a machine allows us to make this trade-off, we say the machine has given us a **mechanical advantage.**

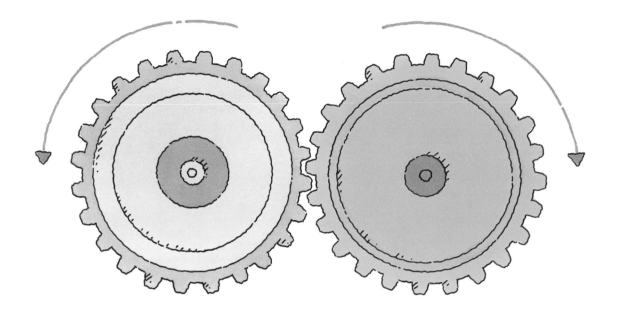

Sometimes, instead of a wheel turning an axle, a wheel turns another wheel. The kinds of wheels that turn other wheels are called **gears.** You can find gears inside many machines, such as wind-up watches, automobiles, and washing machines. They have teeth on their rims. The teeth on one gear push the teeth on another gear. In this way, one gear turns another.

When two gears are turning, the first gear turns the second gear in the opposite direction. When a gear is turning in the same direction as the hands of a clock, we say it is turning **clockwise.** When a gear is turning in the opposite direction, we say it is turning **counterclockwise.**

Imagine that one gear, turning clockwise, turns a second gear in the opposite direction, or counterclockwise. Can you see why adding a third gear would change the direction back to the clockwise motion of the original gear?

A gear fastened to a vertical axle can be used to turn a gear that is fastened to a horizontal axle. Often the teeth of the gears are cut at an angle so that they can mesh more easily. This gives us a change in the direction of force.

Gears not only change the direction in which wheels turn, they also change the speed at which they turn. When a larger gear turns a smaller gear, the smaller gear turns faster than the larger gear. When a smaller gear turns a larger gear, the larger gear turns slower than the smaller gear.

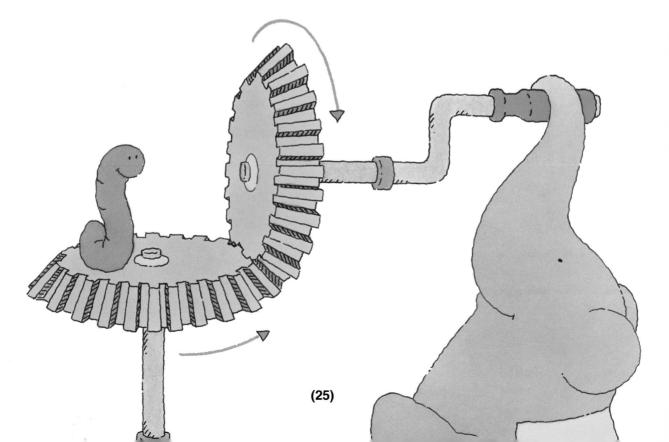

Gears can also change the amount of force with which a wheel turns. When a larger gear makes a smaller gear turn faster, the smaller gear also turns with less force than the larger gear. When a smaller gear makes a larger gear turn slower, the larger gear has more force than the smaller gear. This relationship between the force of the smaller and the larger gears is the mechanical advantage.

One way to observe how gears operate is to look at a 10-speed bike. Bikes have special gears known as **sprocket gears.** Sprocket gears don't touch one another. Instead they are connected by a chain with holes in it. The teeth on the rim of the gears fit into the holes. When one gear turns, it pulls the chain, and the chain makes the other gear turn.

When you ride a bike with gears, can you feel the
mechanical advantage that you gain as you change
gears? When you get more power to go up a hill, where
are you giving more distance? Why can you pedal more
slowly on a flat road in "high" gear and still go faster
than you went up the hill in "low" gear?

Look around at the room you are in. Do you think you can count all the wheels? You probably can't. You'd have to open all the machines and peer inside where many wheels are hidden.

Wheels and axles can be tricky to spot since they can show up where you least expect them. What does this eggbeater remind you of? And the notched wheel that's used to cut this pizza into slices?

How many wheels and axles can you see in this picture? If you find it hard to imagine how devices so different in shape and size can all function as wheels and axles, repeat the experiment using the pencil and the lid. Try to spot the similar parts.

Look around you indoors and out. There are
wheels all over the place. It wouldn't be too far from the
truth to say that wheels make the world go 'round!

Index / Glossary

Axle: the rod that connects to a wheel to form a simple machine, 11.

Ball bearing: a ball placed between the moving parts of a machine, 10.

Complex machine: a machine made up of combinations of simple machines, 12.

Force: the effort applied to move something, 13.

Friction: the force that resists the movement of two objects touching each other, 9.

Gear: a wheel with teeth on its rim, 6.

Mechanical advantage: the relationship between the effort you put into the machine and the force you get out of it, 22.

Simple machine: a device that allows us to reduce the amount of effort we use to do work, 11.

Trade-off: the exchange between distance and force that occurs when we do work, 19.

Work: force times distance equals work, 13.